Mommy's Gummies

A children's educational cannabis book

By Hans Vargas

Copyright © 2021 by Hans Vargas. All rights reserved.

No part of this publication may be reproduced, stored in a retrieval system, or transmitted in any form, or by any means, electronic, mechanical, photocopying, recording, or otherwise, without written permission of the author.

This book is a work of fiction. Any references to historical events, real people, or real places are used fictitiously. Other names, characters, places, and events are products of the author's imagination, and any resemblance to actual events or places or persons, living or dead, is entirely coincidental.

ISBN 978-1-7771486-7-6 (e-book)
ISBN 978-1-7771486-6-9 (hardcover)

Published by Kallpa Publishing Inc.
Visit us at www.kallpapub.com

Vargas, Hans
Mommy's Gummies

It's a sunny Saturday morning. Kiara wakes up very early, and super excited, because it's her birthday!

Kiara will be five today and she is so happy because her friends are coming to celebrate her birthday.

Kiara looks everywhere for her presents while mommy and daddy are sleeping.

While looking in the pantry, Kiara notices a bag full of Gummy Bears.

Kiara is so happy to find Gummy Bears because they are her favorites! She takes the bag and goes straight to watch TV.

Kiara starts to feel dizzy. "MOMMY!!!!" she cries.

Mommy and Daddy find Kiara and see her on the floor, sweating and crying, holding the bag of Gummy Bears. They are so worried.

Daddy reaches for his phone and calls the poison hotline. He says, "my five-year-old daughter has taken cannabis gummy bears!!! What do I do?!!!!"

The lady at the poison center explains in a calm voice, "please, calm down and take your daughter to the nearest hospital. Everything will be alright."

Kiara's Mommy and Daddy arrive at the hospital and are greeted by Doctor Ruth. She asks them to please calm down, and that everything will be alright.

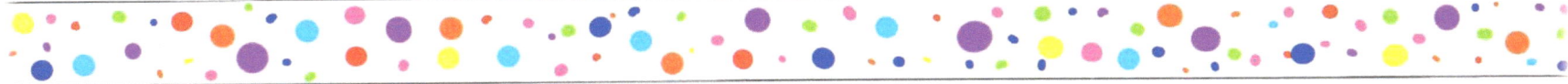

Doctor Ruth sits Kiara on a hospital bed and hands her a glass of orange juice. Meanwhile, she reassures Kiara that she will start to feel much better.

Doctor Ruth meets Kiara's parents and explains that Kiara will be fine, but cannabis gummies must be locked away from children.

Doctor Ruth asks Mommy, Daddy and Kiara to please sit down and to listen to her clearly. Children should never eat anything without asking mommy and daddy what that is.

On the way home, Kiara promised Mommy and Daddy that she will never ever take anything without asking first.

Then, they all hugged and walked home to enjoy Kiara's birthday party.

Medical cannabis has been slowly been accepted by many governments around the world. Unfortunately, both the government and adults consumers need to find a way to teach children about the temptations of taking candy that is medicated with cannabis extracts, and we also need to inform adults that they should keep all these legal medical products, alongside other opioids, in a locked space away from children.

There is still much to learn about the psychoactive effects of cannabis and how to reduce them. In this tale, Doctor Ruth gives us an example with orange juice as this drink can slowly diminish the THC psychoactive effects.

Since the legalization of cannabis, many adults and children have fallen into the trap of the sweet flavoured infused candy and other type of modified foods. In consequence, hospitals were overwhelmed with many patients that came in with panic and anxiety. Fortunately, it is only an effect that will last for a few hours and will not cause any life-threatening situations. Doctors are aware of this.

Continue fighting the stigma.

www.ingramcontent.com/pod-product-compliance
Lightning Source LLC
Chambersburg PA
CBHW041108210426

43209CB00063BA/1857